Beyond Repair:
Section 609's Magic Path to Credit Redemption

Erase Derogatory Accounts Fast In 30 Days With a Proven Legal Strategy

By
SEAN MONTES

Copyright © 2017* . 2019-2022

Table of Contents

Legal Notes 4
The Reason It Works 4
What To Expect 4
Getting Started Cleaning Up Your Credit 4
Dispute Letters 4
Level 1 Dispute Letter Template 4
Level 2 Dispute Letter Template 4
Level 3 Dispute Letter Template 4
Level 4 Dispute Letter Template 4
Conclusion 4
Introduction 1

1
2
3
5
7
8
9
12
15
18
21

Introduction

The Fair Credit Reporting Act Section 609 could have been a lifesaver for me if I had known about it earlier. My credit issues caused me a lot of stress and worry, and I believe that this provision would have saved me years of my life. Nonetheless, I hope you come across this information sooner rather than later, but even if you do not, it will still work wonders for you.

It is quite simple to heal your credit, and you can do so without any external assistance. This guidebook provides you with the necessary knowledge to achieve this goal on your own. By following the steps outlined in this book, you can regain control of your credit score and improve your life.

Having a good credit score is crucial in many aspects of life. It can determine whether you are eligible for a decent apartment, utilities, phone, cable, internet services, car or house loans with good rates, and credit cards that offer rewards for purchases. Therefore, your FICO score is a significant financial tool that can either benefit or harm you. I hope that your FICO score will help you in all future endeavors.

Kindly take note of the following text without expecting a response from me: "I have an eBook that contains letters to aid you in improving your credit score. These letters are uncomplicated and direct, and most importantly, they have proven to be effective. However, the outcome may vary depending on your unique situation, and may require several iterations of letter writing.

However, persistently using this method to dispute all negative accounts in your credit report will eventually help restore your credit. So, keep using this approach until your credit is spotless, and your FICO score is at the desired level."

Legal Notes

This book may not be reproduced or transferred in any form without written permission from the author.

The accuracy and completeness of the information provided here are not guaranteed or warranted to produce any particular results, and the advice and/or strategies contained within may or may not be suitable for every individual.

The author shall not be liable for any losses incurred as a consequence of the use and application of any information presented in this book, either directly or indirectly.

The author of this book has made a sincere effort to present the subject matter in detail. However, it is important to note that the book is offered for sale with a disclaimer, stating that the author does not offer any accounting, legal, or other professional services. Therefore, if you require any legal counseling or expert assistance, it is recommended that you seek the services of a qualified professional.

The Reason It Works

The three major credit reporting agencies known as CRAs are Equifax, Experian, and TransUnion. These names will become familiar to you in the future if they are not already. Essentially, whenever you engage in any credit-related activity with a bank or credit card company, such as using a credit card or applying for a loan, the CRAs typically receive and record this information in your credit report, which is linked to your Social Security Number.

It is worth noting that all reporting is carried out digitally, and there is no paper trail to follow. There are no signed papers or contracts that have been verified in any way. Banks and credit card issuers automatically send computerized files containing account information to credit reporting agencies every month; this information is included in the credit report without any verification. No one is checking to see if you own the account, or if the data is accurate. Additionally, there is no oversight to ensure that the creditors or banks act ethically.

It is noteworthy that credit reporting agencies Equifax, Experian, and TransUnion believe that the reports submitted by credit card companies is accurate. Although this may be true, it cannot be confirmed without further verification. To address this issue, the US government enacted the Fair Credit Reporting Act (FCRA), which serves as a law for credit reporting agencies. As an American citizen, your rights are protected by this legislation. According to the FCRA, the bureaus must verify any information before including it in your credit report by checking with banks, credit card companies, and other sources. The original signed document from when you applied for a loan or opened a credit card is what CRAs need to see. However, it is impossible and costly to verify the paperwork for millions of accounts, so this process is not being followed.

It is important to note that there is no verification process in place to authenticate the original signed contract documents between the credit reporting agencies and creditors. If one were to request verification, the credit bureaus would simply send an electronic message to the creditor asking if the information is correct, to which the creditor would most likely reply with a "Yes." However, no physical inspection of the original signed contracts was conducted.

There is a little-known fact that only a few people are aware of now, including yourself. The Credit Reporting Agencies (CRAs) are violating the Fair Credit Reporting Act (FCRA), but because most individuals are unaware of their rights, CRAs are not held accountable for their actions.

It is important to keep in mind that disputing negative items in credit reports through the traditional dispute resolution process may not always be effective. Many of the negative statements in your report may be accurate and verified, which can ultimately lead to a lower FICO score.

This is not what you are trying to do. Do not ever dispute your credit report online.

It is worth noting that under SECTION 609 of the Fair Credit Reporting Act, the validity of a negative account is not relevant. In a dispute letter, the focus should be on questioning the credit reporting agency's authority to report the adverse account rather than disputing the account's validity itself. SECTION 609 of the Fair

Credit Reporting Act does not consider whether a negative account is valid or not. The letter disputes the CRA's right to REPORT the adverse account – NOT–whether the adverse account is valid.

Under SECTION 609 of the Fair Credit Reporting Act, these letters will request that the CRAs are required to provide a copy of the original contract that you signed since they are supposed to have it when verifying the validity of the account. However, I noticed that they do not ever have a copy of the contract, which means that they cannot provide it to us or legally verify the account. As per the Fair Credit Reporting Act, they must provide us with a copy of the contract if we request it. However, because they cannot, the account remains unverified, and according to Federal Law, any unverified accounts must be deleted.

It is also worth noting that the results obtained from disputing accounts may differ depending on the number of accounts that need to be disputed. You could send just one round of letters and have everything removed, or it may take up to four rounds to get everything removed. Persistence is key here: keep sending those letters and be prepared to go a few rounds before resolving.

What To Expect

It is important to keep in mind that when you send off your notarized letters to Experian, TransUnion, and Equifax, they may choose to ignore or intimidate you in an attempt to deter you from continuing your dispute. They might even send you a reply stating that a suspicious letter was sent on your behalf but has been ignored. Despite these challenges, it is crucial to persevere and keep pushing forward.

I have personally seen this response.

"We received a suspicious request regarding your personal credit information that we have determined was not sent by you. We have not taken any action on this request and any future requests made in this manner will not be processed and will not receive a response."

It is important to note that any letter sent will be notarized and tracked. If you wish to expedite the process, sending it via priority mail is the best option. Priority mail comes with tracking and typically takes only a few days to reach the CRA, as opposed to weeks. Additionally, each letter includes a copy of your Social Security Card and Driver's license. However, if the CRA claims that they did not receive a letter from you, this raises the question of how they came to that conclusion.

They didn't. This is just a scare tactic. So, hear me out – KEEP GOING.

You may even get something like this:

"Suspicious requests are taken seriously and reviewed by our security personnel who will report deceptive activity, including copies of letters deemed as suspicious, to law enforcement officials and to state or federal regulatory agencies."

It's just another one of their scare tactics. They may also ask for proof of your identity and request that you mail them such proof. However, you have already sent a notarized letter with your SS Card and ID, so what is the problem?

KEEP GOING!

Based on the available information, it seems evident that the party in question is intentionally delaying and attempting to intimidate you. To address this, my recommendation is to send a new round of letters, emphasizing that this is your second (or third or fourth) request, and making it clear that legal action will be pursued if necessary. Continue to demand that Equifax, Experian, and TransUnion properly verify your accounts by providing a signed copy of your original contracts. If they fail to comply with this request, they are obliged to remove any negative accounts from their records.

In the event they ignore you altogether, you can file a lawsuit and sue the bureaus. You can file your complaint here:

https://www.ftccomplaintassistant.gov

Getting Started Cleaning Up Your Credit

In the US, you can get a free credit report once a year from Experian, Equifax, and TransUnion, respectively. This means ifyou haven't checked your credit report in the last 12 months, you could get it for free. To get your reports, you can visit this website:

http://www.annualcreditreport.com.

Once you have your credit reports, you should look for any negative items that may have affected your credit score. These negative items need to be disputed, so it's important to identify them before you can start the dispute process.

First, obtain the dispute letters for Experian, Equifax, and TransUnion. Then, copy the adverse information from your credit reports into the letters and send them to the CRAs. It is important to keep in mind that disputing more than 22 adverse accounts at once could lead to the CRA's categorizing your dispute as frivolous. Therefore, it is recommended that no more than 22 accounts be disputed at a time.

For example, let's say there are eight negative accounts in your TransUnion credit report. Take TransUnion Letter 1, write it up and add the eight accounts you want to remove. Then, do the same for Experian and Equifax: Once you have written the letters, you will need to get them notarized.

You have to make your letter(s) official by getting them notarized. To prove your identity, you need to attach a copy of your social security card and a government-issued ID, such as your driver's license or passport. Remember not to sign the letter(s) until the notary tells you to do so. Once you have done this, your letters are ready to be sent.

You will send your letter WITH TRACKING and the good choices are Priority Mail or Certified Mail. This will be your proof that the CRAs have received your dispute letter(s).

Just be patient and wait for a response in the mail. If the credit bureaus did not remove all negative accounts and did not provide written proof, don't worry. Keep moving forward by sending the next letter in this guide.

I recommend maintaining three folders for each bureau. Remember to submit a dispute to each Credit Reporting Agency and retain all the receipts along with the tracking numbers, copies of the responses, letters sent, and any relevant notes. 1 for each Credit Reporting Agency and keep all the receipts with the tracking numbers, copies of the responses, copies of the letters you send, notes, etc. You are going to need a paper trail because if you need to sue you will need evidence. Hopefully, it does not come to this point, but evidence will be invaluable if such a thing needs to occur.

Dispute Letters

The templates for the dispute letters are as follows: My recommendation would be to handwrite these letters to guarantee that they are viewed by a human and not a machine. Below are the addresses that you will use for the credit bureaus: Equifax, Experian, and TransUnion.

First, you will start by sending a Level 1 letter to all three bureaus. You will then send a Level 2 letter to all three bureaus. Then, a Level 3 letter to all three bureaus. If you still have not received all the adverse accounts off your credit score, you will need to send a Level 4 letter to all three bureaus.

Equifax

P.O. Box 740256

Atlanta, GA 30374

Experian

P.O. Box 2002

Allen, TX 75013

Trans Union

P.O. Box # 2000

Chester, PA. 19022

The Level 1 letter template is below: It consists of two pages. All your letters will be two pages long.

After The Level 1 letter template, next is the Level 2 letter template followed by Level 3 then the Level 4 letter template.

Level 1 Dispute Letter Template

DATE

Your Name

Address

City, State Zip

SSN: 000-00-0000 | DOB: 1/1/1970

CREDIT REPORTING AGENCY PO BOX ADDRESS CITY, STATE ZIP CODE

According to the Fair Credit Reporting Act, Section 609 (a)(1)(A), you are required by federal law to verify

through the physical verification of the original signed consumer contract - any accounts you post on a credit report. Otherwise, anyone paying for your reporting services could fax, mail, or email in a fraudulent account.

I demand to see the Verifiable Proof (an original Consumer Contract with my signature on it) you have on file for the accounts listed below. Your failure to positively verify that these accounts hurt my ability to obtain credit. Under the FCRA, unverified accounts must be removed. If you are unable to provide me with verifiable proof, you must remove the accounts listed below.

I demand that the following accounts be verified or removed immediately.

| Account | Account Number | Provide Physical |

		Verification
Creditor 1	1234567890	Unverified Account
Creditor 2	Etc	Unverified Account
Creditor 3		Unverified Account
Creditor 4		Unverified Account
Creditor 5		Unverified Account
Creditor 6		Unverified Account
Creditor 7		Unverified Account
Creditor 8		Unverified Account
Creditor 9		Unverified Account
Creditor 10		Unverified Account

Please remove all non-account-holding inquiries over 30 days old.

Please add a Promotional Suppression to my credit file.

Thank You,

{YOUR NAME HERE}

IN WITNESS WHEREOF, the said party has signed and sealed these presents the day and year first above written.

Signed, sealed, and delivered in the presence of:

{PRINT YOUR NAME HERE}

_____

Signature

STATE OF COUNTY OF

I HEREBY CERTIFY that on this day before me, an officer duly qualified to take acknowledgments, personally appeared {YOUR NAME HERE}, who has produced

_____

as identification and who executed the foregoing instrument, and he/she acknowledged before me that he/she executed the same.

WITNESS my hand and official seal in the County and State aforesaid this _____ day of_____ 2018.

_____

Notary Public

Printed Name

My commission expires:

COPY OF SSN CARD

COPY OF ID CARD

Level 2 Dispute Letter Template

DATE

Your Name

Address

City, State Zip

SSN: 000-00-0000 | DOB: 1/1/1970

CREDIT REPORTING AGENCY PO BOX ADDRESS CITY, STATE ZIP CODE

Please be advised this is my SECOND WRITTEN REQUEST. The unverified items listed below remain on my credit report in violation of Federal Law. You are required under the FCRA to have a copy of the original creditor's documentation on file to verify that this information is mine and correct. In the results of your first investigation, you stated in writing that you "verified" that these items are being "reported correctly" Who verified these accounts?

You have NOT provided me a copy of ANY original documentation required under Section 609 (a)(1)(A) & Section 611 (a)(1)(A) (a consumer contract with my signature on it) and Section 611 (5)(A) of the FCRA – you are required to

"…promptly DELETE all information which cannot be verified."

The law is very clear as to the Civil liability and the remedy available to me for "negligent noncompliance" (Section 617,) if you fail to comply. I am a litigious consumer and fully intend to pursue litigation in this matter to enforce my rights under the FCRA *.

I demand that the following accounts be verified or deleted immediately.

Account	Account Number	Provide Physical Verification
Creditor 1	1234567890	Unverified Account
Creditor 2	Etc	Unverified Account
Creditor 3		Unverified Account
Creditor 4		Unverified Account
Creditor 5		Unverified Account
Creditor 6		Unverified Account

Please remove all non-account-holding inquiries over 30 days old.

Please add a Promotional Suppression to my credit file.

Thank You,

{YOUR NAME HERE}

IN WITNESS WHEREOF, the said party has signed and sealed these presents the day and year first above written.

Signed, sealed, and delivered in the presence of:

{PRINT YOUR NAME HERE}

_____

Signature

STATE OF COUNTY OF

I HEREBY CERTIFY that on this day before me, an officer duly qualified to take acknowledgments, personally appeared { YOUR NAME HERE }, who has produced

_____

as identification and who executed the foregoing instrument, and he/she acknowledged before me that he/she executed the same.

WITNESS my hand and official seal in the County and State aforesaid this _____ day of_____ 2018.

_____

Notary Public

Printed Name

My commission expires:

```
┌─────────────────────────────┐
│                             │
│     COPY OF SSN CARD        │
│                             │
└─────────────────────────────┘


┌─────────────────────────────┐
│                             │
│     COPY OF ID CARD         │
│                             │
└─────────────────────────────┘
```

Level 3 Dispute Letter Template

DATE

Your Name

Address

City, State Zip

SSN: 000-00-0000 | DOB: 1/1/1970

CREDIT REPORTING AGENCY PO BOX ADDRESS CITY, STATE ZIP CODE

Please be advised that this is my THIRD WRITTEN REQUEST and FINAL WARNING that I fully intend to pursue litigation by the FCRA to enforce my rights and seek relief and recover all monetary damages that I may be entitled to under Sections 616 and 617 regarding your continued willful and negligent noncompliance.

Despite two written requests, the unverified items listed below remain on my credit report in violation of Federal Law. You are required under the FCRA to have a copy of the original creditor's documentation on file to verify that this information is mine and is correct. The results of your first investigation and subsequent reinvestigation, you stated in writing that you "verified" that these items are being "reported correctly" Who verified these accounts? You have NOT provided me with a copy of ANY original documentation (a consumer contract with my signature on it) as required under Section 609 (a)(1)(A) and Section 611 (a)(1)(A). Furthermore, you failed to provide the verification method required in Sections 611 (a) and (7). Please be advised that under Section 611 (5)(A) of the FCRA – you are required to "...*promptly DELETE all information which cannot be verified.*"

The law is very clear as to the civil liability and the remedy available to me (Sections 616 and 617) if you fail to comply with Federal Law. I am a litigious consumer and fully intend to pursue litigation in this matter to enforce my rights under the FCRA.

I demand that the following accounts be verified or deleted immediately.

Account	Account Number	Provide Physical Verification
Creditor 1	1234567890	Unverified Account
Creditor 2	Etc	Unverified Account
Creditor 3		Unverified Account
Creditor 4		Unverified Account

Please remove all non-account-holding inquiries over 30 days old.

Please add a Promotional Suppression to my credit file.

Thank You,

{YOUR NAME HERE}

IN WITNESS WHEREOF, the said party has signed and sealed these presents the day and year first above written.

Signed, sealed, and delivered in the presence of:

{PRINT YOUR NAME HERE}

_____

Signature

STATE OF COUNTY OF

I HEREBY CERTIFY that on this day before me, an officer duly qualified to take acknowledgments, personally appeared {YOUR NAME HERE}, who has produced

_____

as identification and who executed the foregoing instrument, and he/she acknowledged before me that he/she executed the same.

WITNESS my hand and official seal in the County and State aforesaid this _____ day of_____ 2018.

_____

Notary Public

Printed Name

My commission expires:

[COPY OF SSN CARD]

[COPY OF ID CARD]

Level 4 Dispute Letter Template

DATE

Your Name

Address

City, State Zip

SSN: 000-00-0000 | DOB: 1/1/1970 CREDIT

REPORTING AGENCY

PO BOX ADDRESS

CITY, STATE ZIP CODE

NOTICE OF PENDING LITIGATION SEEKING RELIEF AND MONETARY DAMAGES UNDER FCRA SECTION 616 & SECTION 617 Please accept this final written OFFER OF SETTLEMENT BEFORE LITIGATION as my attempt to amicably resolve your continued violation of the Fair Credit Reporting Act regarding your refusal to delete UNVERIFIED information from my consumer file.

I intend to pursue litigation by the FCRA to seek relief and recover all monetary damages that I may be entitled to under Sections 616 and 617 if the UNVERIFIED items listed below are not deleted immediately. A copy of this letter, as well as copies of the three written letters sent to you previously, will also become part of a formal complaint to the Federal Trade Commission and shall be used as evidence in pending litigation provided you fail to comply with this offer of settlement.

Despite three written requests, the unverified items listed below remain on my credit report in violation of Federal Law. You are required under the FCRA to have a copy of the original creditor's documentation on file to verify that this information is mine and correct. In the results of your investigations, you stated in writing that you "verified" that these items are being "reported correctly" Who verified these accounts? You have NOT provided me with a copy of ANY original documentation (a consumer contract with my signature on it) as required under Section 609 (a)(1)(A) and Section 611 (a)(1)(A). Furthermore, you have failed to provide the method of verification as required under Section 611 (a)(7). Please be advised that under Section 611 (5)(A) of the FCRA – you are required to "...*promptly DELETE all information which cannot be verified.*"

The law is very clear as to the Civil liability and the remedy available to me (Section 616 & 617) if you fail to comply with Federal Law. I am a litigious consumer and fully intend to pursue litigation in this matter to enforce my rights under the FCRA.

I demand that the following accounts be verified or deleted immediately.

Account	Account Number	Provide Physical Verification
Creditor 1	1234567890	Unverified Account
Creditor 2	Etc	Unverified Account
Creditor 3		Unverified

Creditor 4	Account
Unverified
Account

Please remove all non-account-holding inquiries over 30 days old.

* Please add a Promotional Suppression to my credit file.

Thank You,

{YOUR NAME HERE}

IN WITNESS WHEREOF, the said party has signed and sealed these presents the day and year first above written.

Signed, sealed, and delivered in the presence of:

{PRINT YOUR NAME HERE}

_____

Signature

STATE OF COUNTY OF

I HEREBY CERTIFY that on this day before me, an officer duly qualified to take acknowledgments, personally appeared {YOUR NAME HERE}, who has produced

_____

as identification and who executed the foregoing instrument, and he/she acknowledged before me that he/she executed the same.

WITNESS my hand and official seal in the County and State aforesaid this _____ day of_____ 2018.

_____

Notary Public

Printed Name

My commission expires:

```
┌─────────────────────────────┐
│                             │
│     COPY OF SSN CARD        │
│                             │
└─────────────────────────────┘
```

```
┌─────────────────────────────┐
│                             │
│     COPY OF ID CARD         │
│                             │
└─────────────────────────────┘
```

Conclusion

This process will work. You will have to stay on top of all the dispute letters, but this will also improve your FICO score, so please, please, please, stay on it. I know it is not the easiest thing to do to type up all your letters, but it will be worth it!

Thank you so very much for trusting me with your credit health!

Wishing you the best,

Sean